Distractables

A Super Cute Very Nice Coloring Book

illustrated by:
KATIE DAUGHERTY & BREE LUNDBERG

Free Period Press
www.freeperiodpress.com
ISBN 978-0-9909144-9-5
© 2016 Free Period Press LLC

We'd love to see your finished artwork! Tag your photos using #freeperiodpress

KATIE
DAUGHERTY

illustrator

KATIE
DAUGHERTY

illustrator

KATIE
DAUGHERTY

illustrator

Little Nugget of Truth

"You look great today!"

DECODE the MESSAGE

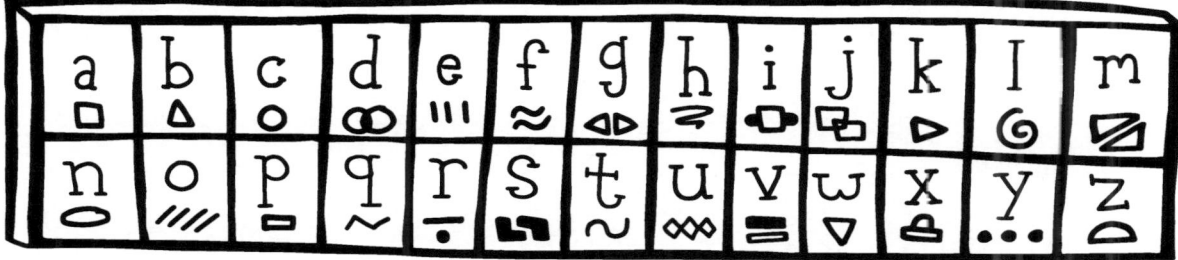

USE THIS DECODER TO REVEAL A VERY REAL TRUTH.

KATIE
DAUGHERTY

illustrator

KATIE DAUGHERTY

illustrator

OMG OMG OMG
OMG OMG OMG
OMG OMG OMG
OMG OMG OMG
OMG OMG OMG
OMG OMG OMG

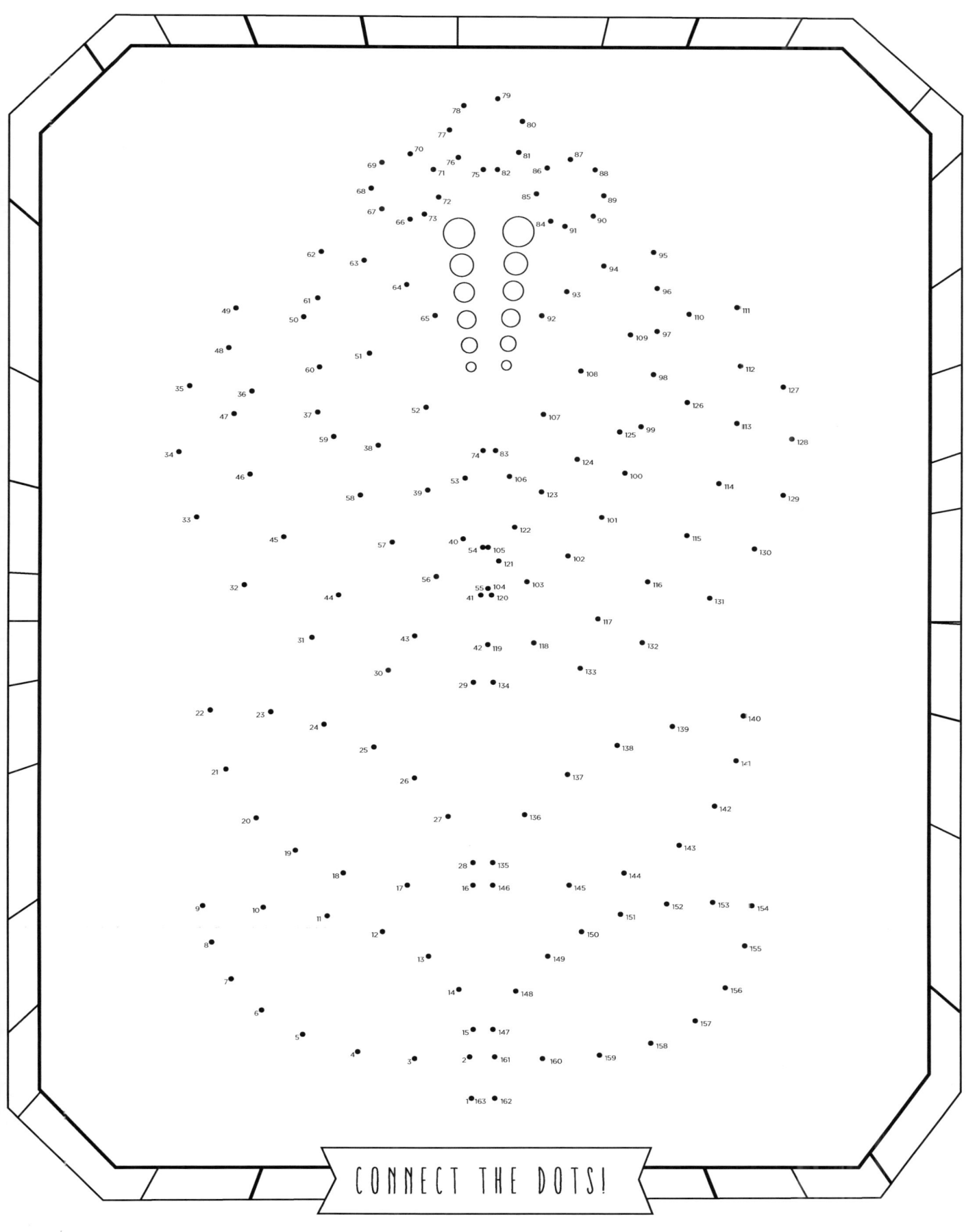

CONNECT THE DOTS!

KATIE
DAUGHERTY

---
illustrator